CITY *of* WATER

CITY *of* WATER
Robert Thompson

*aha***dada**

books

TOKYO · TORONTO

LIBRARY OF CONGRESS ISBN 978-0-9808873-3-4
FIRST PRINTING: JANUARY, 2009   LIMITED TO 500 COPIES

dedicated to
Lauren and Owen Thompson

I want to thank Anne Noonan for the design of CITY OF WATER and Jessie Glass of *aha*dada press for his friendship and encouragement.

CONTENTS

A BEAUTIFUL LIFE

One wonders about the rose-thorn waterfalls,
slippery mossy boulders, cantilevered these millennia,
what swarm of sprites,
what clever draftsman and backhoe guy
pushed and knocked it out?
One envies the earth, its illimitable creations,
or admires the earth but envies those who
merely need glance or touch for treasures to gush up.
Who gets to walk in beauty? You with your shaded lawns,
your pine-needle paths and surprised fauna,
your recessed stone benches by meandering waters,
your verdant inclines and undulant forested views,
your shushing grasses, your jet black pools
your jet-free blue above, your belief in your sovereignty,
as you swish a golf club, which flies from your grip
and lands in the teeth of your employer.

BROOKLYN LANDSCAPE: 24TH AVENUE, BENSONHURST

A twisted, stripped frame of a girl's
(pink pastels amid spots of rust)
bike lies on its side
across the sidewalk. Blown
over by the wind,
it is framed by an actual
picture frame, gold gilt,
large enough to step into
and bathe, or to contain
an arm-wide panorama
of Sicily. By the garbage cans,
the frame in the frame
blocks the walk,
so you must look at this picture
punctured by broken motion
before someone grabs it
and calls it art.

A MOCKINGBIRD AND A MOSQUITO

A mockingbird outside the bedroom window
and a mosquito inside the screen,
near ears and succulent skin,
replace dreams with daytime worries.
The bird has the trees of this multiplex courtyard
to itself, and I am its captive
audience. The mosquito has us, too,
to itself, and lifts from an itch
on the back of my hand.
Slowly thinking who I am,
I come to the dewy dappled dawn.
Or not. This mystery,
always a page-turner,
will not become clearer this morning
before motion and routine roll in.
The mockingbird mimics
and the mosquito bites, after all,
not to enlighten
but to live.

NEW COSMOLOGY

The pale south-west embalms the sun.
A frolicsome porn star,
known as Ton a Fun,
lap dances across the sky.
Soon the moon stares down
and spits on lewd enterprise.
A man and a woman lie
knotted in the wanton moonlight.
The satellite dish on the rooftop
swallows and transmits
the exact act they exhibit
to the monitor hidden
in their heads. Out of the soupy medium
bobs their replacement,
a new baby God.

THE TIN GARGOYLE

The world quietly turns,
you there, not the world,
the gray skyscrapers steam,
also, manhole covers.
Now, the daily planet
springs, off perspective.
Your blood leaps Up,
Up, and Away.
Tower of earth, your low watt
flourescence, an economy,
perks up the city, then
the sun hogs
the view, lots
of color, and glare galore.
Let me tell you what's true.
I take it back.
The truth about the city,
the truth about the world,
the truth about me
pass by, eyes straight ahead.

THE LIGHT OF THINGS

Believe not the artificial fire, when its redness makes all things look ghastly.
To-morrow, in the natural sun, the skies will be bright. –Herman Melville

The barking begins about an hour before dawn.
"Step right up! Touch the She-that's-a-He!"
"Have a go at this fetching creature: your mothersonsisterstudent!"
Painful to recognize, it mutates at your whim.
Whose body so familiar – ye gads! – familial, is this?
Admit it. The line is to be crossed, pleasure taken,
and shame but a piquant prologue to the proceedings.

Just as this builds to a colossus of death,
a great movie lights up your shade,
accompanied by bird song.
Prepare for the day, pack away the odious props and masks of sleep!
Too much tumult and polymorphous perversity!—
subplot to your waking
steps, the first dozen or so that guide you towards

routine matters, the sanity of immediacy.
So, shave your face without slashing your throat,
bring milk to the hungry boy in the crib,
be a good citizen of the house and companionable mate.

True, you don't always know how to respond to mail or phone calls,
facts as massive as any natural wonders.
The utility bills drop upon you like the falls at Niagara.
A call from a superior darkens your mood more than any storm cloud could.
But when you step back, or to be more accurate, lean into the stroke,
the practical problem bounces from the racket; it is play.
And there is nothing at all above or below this daily exercise.

That is the plausible story, whose ambient strains
whistle like wind across a passing car.
It is on the shaven or just made up faces of your neighbors
who march straight to their daily occupations.
For, unless their jobs are ripped from their hands,
you can count on all points of civility holding firm,
and, effortlessly, everyone not strangling one another.

Then why the "sickly abstractions," as Whitman called them?
Begin with Oma's bible lessons on Armageddon:
You squirmed, glancing from her bedroom onto the Connecticut turnpike,
half wishing for a crash and the ritual red lights.
Satan was battling Jehovah over you, she warned.
This "system of things" would fall like the walls of Jericho.
She had facts. Wasn't the Bomb ever ready to drop?

Didn't a tabloid shriek about a psycho
tossing acid in the Bronx?
Wasn't a feeling for war flashing past peace in Vietnam?
She seemed to know what you, a small boy, could only guess at:
this civil strife, this earthquake, this nasty weather
foretold the end, the winnowing out,
and then—
Paradise, and the lamb and the lion would lie together.

What finally overpowered these scare stories?
Someone, perhaps your father, had jinxed them:
"A professor of mine said religion is the root of all evil."
And your mom, a passive loyalist, let "Oma" do the converting.
Her apocalyptic wrath and lamentations nearly burst the small bedroom,
but the family station wagon was packed up and we moved to a new state.
You cried at leaving her, and she stood waving, waving so-long.

Now at night the notions you shrugged off as her eccentricity
whip around a distant pole called sanity-skepticism
and hurtle back, back, back towards the other pole, lunatic credulity.
Why not entertain fantasies of demon possession?
How else explain the lurid scenarios "someone" thrusts into the mind's eye?
Each baseless fear needs only a slight clutch of believers to thrive,
and one "perhaps" to unseat the calm and sagacious adult in you,
send him tumbling headfirst into a puddle of his own blood.
But here is the thing itself, not as funny as Irving's headless horseman
and not just a youthful melodrama prompted by pot.
For a few seconds, you feel a shift in the orbit
by which you have come to think, perceive, and express,
a shift which has a sudden, psychotic wobble.
The wobble increases, but just before chaos prevails, you breath,

the simple act God needed to see
before lifting you from the path of this remote, invisible calamity.
Or, a huge obsession, your pumping heart.
You wake and it is again erratic, a timepiece unsprung,
and with eyes closed you count beats, but cannot regulate it.
Gradually, a vast throbbing emanates outside you, indeed,
outside your bedroom, and even outside your family's house.

You have awakened early in the morning in a suburb in the Midwest,
and a giant heart pounds slowly behind the horizon of frame houses,
above the shadowed lives of families whose crises emerge suddenly
and then, drop to the volume at which shame forces them to abide.
With your bedroom window open to the south and the birds stilled yet,
you hear a deep, step-like concussion and conclude that this is your doom,
when the fear in your mind has migrated to the real outside.

The sound is for once so clearly outside your interior theater
that you are both terrified and relieved to witness the event,

though, unlike the prophet and the burning, talking bush,
it almost embarrasses you, like the moment actors in a modern play
climb off the proscenium stage to holler and speechify amid the audience,
so everyone can see their wattles, their rouged cheeks, and puffed bellies.
Yet, you exult because now a fear has become a fact.

What could be more garish than the fantasies of a neurotic teenager?
To catalogue and analyze them would be to snorkel in a cesspool,
a thankless task at the end of which is the scientist's only balm,
fact and theory. What will come of it, he can't say,
a microchip to regulate testosterone for boys,
a regimen of meditation for girls,
or nothing but a humble suspicion and hope.

Clumsy explanations and dubious prescriptions issue from the oracles,
and soon you possess an amber container of pills,
and the unlucky streak you had been on begins to seem strictly O.K.,
but no orgasm of joy unfolds for you either. Your petition has been heard
by the gods, and your case has been assigned to a specialist
whose last case involved a glacier that believed it was retreating.
There was nothing to be done but to make it feel better about this fact.

You decide to take a walk in the municipally owned fields
where trees are strategically stationed to resemble a rural landscape,
or to deflect your perceptions from the din and geometry of the city.
A branch from one of them, a sycamore, has broken and lies in pieces,
but the body above it looks none the worse, probably even lighter, happier.
A conclusion can be drawn about loss and about survival.
The branch, however, will be sawn up and removed by groundskeepers,

and this lesson become just a hymn to civic neatness.
The branch could have fallen unpredictably, of course, crushing a walker,
which would almost compensate for the vast security of it all,

the pond edge that seems to have been traced with a very sharp pencil,
a hill that is no more a result of geology than is the onion dome on a bank.
The lies of the land rise up to condemn and, to be fair, bless you
as you pause before a new waterfall, a thin patch of grass taking root,

a silvery chain link fence behind which ducks waddle towards crumbs.
You breath the air across which jet airplanes leave contrails,
which carries the crude language of sirens and car horns,
and which at this time of day begins blue but ends in a band of dirty orange.
But this is not the beauty for which you set out, or that the landscaper
designed. This is not the true sight but one filtered through sour-tinted lens,
and when you adjust for this given, the agonizing rapids
churn for their space and suddenly die into a meandering swoon
of contentment. A feeling of staring into the Grand Canyon suffuses you
though you but gaze onto a park and a procession of trees in autumn twilight.
You are grateful to accompany the little boy who has not yet seen a thing,
from whose stroller come exclamations at the sunset, at the bee "right there!"
A philosophical system was built once on such as he,
who sits on the edge of his seat when a pigeon or a gull swoops past.

In this park is a cemetery, fenced against trespassers.
It spreads over a wooded hill that looks over the ball fields of a long meadow.
When you walk around the base of this hilly graveyard, you contemplate
the gentle dead and the landscape that secludes them. But you do not grieve.
As usual, you continue on your mildly divided way,
as if you had withdrawn a complaint, and life
had then begun to express itself as it wished.

SOUNDS ON SOUNDS

On the street, the word is "What?"
An airplane drops a propulsive whistle
between a mother and her son,
who sees only lips move and head wag.
For two utility guys, a Brooklyn bellow
becomes just pantomime
against a down-shifting dump truck.
And this morning, a cardinal
chirped its two silver notes
over and over to Owen, our one year old,
until a helicopter droned.
Even to myself, I ask "what?"
and just hear noise.

THE CHAIN

Only one thing was happening.
It was enough to organize oneself around.
The populace skirted it fluently.
A unitary feeling suffused one's movements.

Another thing happened.
It added spice.
It was like an ornamental explosion,
which became its own modality.

Then everything happened at once.
They called it "a cascade effect."
While in it, events cascade headlong
into someplace else. But where?

Here, a shore,
waiting for the tide.

WHITE

The artist leans against the white wall of his studio;
a transistor radio spews its AM radio rhubarb;
he sees the large canvas on wall;
chimes and a fake telegraph play as time and weather.

In the back of the artist's studio, a toilet flushes, muffled;
On the news, nothing new;
the canvas studied is white;
the AM news announcer, also white.

The artist dips brush in paint and tastes;
the AM radio crackles from atmospheric static;
a fume enhances the artist's vision;
the radio station broadcasts a patriotic strain.

In the morning light, bright white, drips of light;
on the transistor radio, an even, unceasing susurration;
the artist stands in view, goggle-eyed, copiously cow-licked;
a melody erupts from the hiss: a Straus waltz.

The artist hears his name on the station
and paints his transistor radio onto the white canvas
and whistles along with the waltz
on a radio not bought for fidelity.

OUT OF IT

Living in a dream, you
seal the compartment. It is tightly shut.
Away from earth, you were deprived.
Now, the earth is upon you.
Hear the faint song of an engine?
It is your mind at ease.
You turn over to give your side some blood.
The people outside the compartment,
and the agencies of nature outside,
leave you alone but idle.
They perform routines plotted by your gaze.
Like an architect, you simply decide.
Then you glance out, amazed at the close
of the shutters of the day.

THE TOT'S PROGRESS

Far from Truth or
myth, the resplendent real
cavorts on the carpet,
a babe, our own, Owen.
Ten months in the world,
ten months its master,
master of table tops
(clear them all!)
master of corners and privileged recesses
(open sesame!)
master of our moods
(follow me in my whims!)
and surely most master of hope and future.
Or like a magnetic field
upsetting notions of north
is Owen looming near,
tiny boy on a woven field of flowers.

* * *

Owen, so cheerful to see me this morning,
bouncing in your crib, still delighted
by your mobile menagerie, enthusiast
of Familia cereal, and of everything
real this morning, I wish you always
to sleep so deeply and so well,
that each turn of the page of your day
surprises you and leads you to such smiles.

NURSE AND PATIENT

For a third day, he lay in bed,
kneeled once in awhile to moan and cough.
I dabbed his nose, gave water or juice.
He sank down again onto his belly, flushed,
panting, dizzy-eyed.
On television, congress was jousting
over no small matter: the impeachment of Clinton.
I wanted to join the fray, dispatch the letter
that would shatter the fallacies that prance
like glass steeds before the battle line.
But that is not my duty.
Today, honorably, I sit beside my baby boy,
and like a woman, like my mother did for me,
cool his fever.

WHO'S AFRAID OF BAUDELAIRE?

I awaken from a guilty nap,
the curses and sneers of Baudelaire
snuffed by a dripping faucet.
I open my green-cloth journal
and write with a curly-cue hand:
"The indominatable weather,
gloomy, pouring, urban, suffocates
my childish will to flourish."
I come to a full stop.
The plastic clock ticks,
the refrigerator hums high and fast,
the slushy tires plane down the street:
They say, It is harmless.
"Harmless," I repeat,
and drop back asleep.

SMALL CROWD, BIG HALL

Diminished to a claque
they sit, slabs.
The dome retracts
and doves elope.
A torch
in a blink of an eye
flashes on empty stands.
A garden of fireworks
grows in the sky.
From this pit,
and from that pit,
players arise.
The claque sounds.
Beautiful bodies
smack into each other.
Dislocations ensue.
A ball wobbles out of play,
bounces about by itself.
An usher ambles after it,
snuggles it,
lets out its air.
One man yawns
in the back of the stands.

now ends. The clouds switch
teams again. Now they are with sunshine
and blue sky, more popular
and more successful. Failed artists
hang their frames
on the museum wall, plaques marked
"Naples and Vesuvius" or just
"Clouds and Cliffs." God, I'd like to
praise a golden ginkgo, only I mean
a light green one, getting yellow, yellower every
single day, until this morning
the sun, no longer needed,
stays abed, leaving bright ginkgo
to pick up the pieces.

FOUR A.M.

A bottle collector carries his bags
under the street light moon,

Clinking glass and rattling cans
preempting the city haulers.

I dreamt of carrying Grandpa to a car
his heart nervously racing
afraid of leaving, I guess.

I buckled us in the seat together,
Dad, hands on the wheel, looking solemnly on.

TEXAS KIN

"I drove out to see the bluebells.
I believe it was the most beautiful thing
I have ever seen," the late "Bob"
of Thompson's Specialties said.

A length of fire hose becomes a hollowed out branch.
Procreant water and sonorous air.
Deserting the store
and the plains, my Dad, "Bobby," bassoons east
to New Haven.

Back at the ranch
style home, Odessa, West Texas,
the vinegarones and tarantulas
play...the short, prickly lawn.

Pumpjacks
black or umber
bob everywhere in the "fields"
once the sea, everywhere sea.

SISTER

in catatonic
squalor:
get out of bed
and pace the rows
of asylum roses
whose petals line
their beds.
You act limbless,
a frozen weed.
Or a stem,
mediate to all things.

CHOKED UP BY TREES

I can't describe the clouds parting
or the disagreements
on our surface.
While you were plucking your eyebrows
I was here, letting our shrill edge
decay. This tree
frightens me with its methods.
Have you ever stood under it and followed
the sequence of its leaves,
the shiver of the bark? When they fulfill
it, I am quiet, as if in comprehension.
There is an unbelievable turn
of veins and channels.
Perhaps if we lock privates,
or you run yours through my hair
like this wind in the boughs,
almost dividing like it, the affection
will precede us. A bird
swoops into being. The late
shadow of its form
pitches itself along the ground
towards trees taken
as uncluttered and unvased,
which you admire. I feel,
though I will not count rings
to verify this. You are arrayed
so green in your demeanor,
I settle under the overhang
and accept your imposition
on the blue.

THE LACHRYMATORY

Reason has begun a crystal
sentence, which, once done,
deserts the premises.
Uncorked dreck whips
from a dervish purgation,
off which you lounge
on pumped up bladders, slurping
flamingo-tinged dregs.
An epistle rubs you raw,
tanning on the rocks,
and call the sun "a bitch."
Tight little reptiles fan out
like our circulatory system
when popped by a bullet:
"fan of blood." Your breath,
after gloving and ungloving,
is the same product, dusty
from an endless shelf-life.

MY LIFE IN THE TREES

Speaking for trees becomes
a yearning to be them.
A light that one lets off
leads to me with a panting grin.
My mother's eyes are that green.
Everytime, it seems, an army
marches off, woods, too
are involved.
I might be in them, afraid
of what they house
or dumb-founded by their air
of having once, and never again, spoken.
Politely, I think tree thoughts.
Their lucubrations on rain
circulate deviously
through thirst
and unfurl to my tacit proposals.

ROOM WITH RED ANDES

Welcome to kindergarten
                          spilt

                    aw

                              spilt

ribbons
            tumble.
the crawling hand.
            the head rolls
                          over roots
                                to trunk base.
welkin, "sky vault"
        lignum, "wood, or tree" or
peace in the pasture
                    lambs sleeping by sun boulders
save one
        the hard rock lamb
                          "am I a lamb? shit if I am"
the crows know
            their parts
                          straighten their pleats.
in the great grass
            lodged in a snail shell
                    father programs
                          past candle light
                                morning
lighter blue
            than the screen.
blinders on, ploughs
            through data
        arresting:
            the field:
resumes display.
                          poor kid
                                listens.
bitten off more than you can Chew?

       recite ten lines of,
the procedure of,
           the names of,
and do.
     DO.
        Peasblossom.
               Cynthia.
                     Eloquentia.

Terminator.

I, whilst napping in the shade of the last elm, had steal upon me my treacherous other, who placed behind my nether lip a windowpane of acid. When I awoke, waking was as sleep, sleep was vanquished, and I wandered dreaming and yet all awake to myself.

I wondered indeed
     in view of the world
         decisively oerlooking the falls
           roaring in their pit

A crowd too gawks at the falls. A woman rails, "Why don't you jump then! I'm sick of your whining," and her teenager sags. We turn, sickened by the churning tears. A cry, and we glimpse the slight figure go down. The woman curses, and the confusion and indignation of the witnesses drown out the rumble of the waters.

         and sought gentle rebuke
       and termed
slightly pendulous
    heavily tilting
        recumbent
          a measure
       really definite
so exact that witnesses queue out the hall

and along the sidewalk, cold withstanding,
     shivering at prospects
         they will be entertained!
            they thrill to plucked strings
               enlarged to meet the greater need
                    for plucked strings
                         voices push far ahead
                   so roof beams quiver
               in the auditorium
            lounge area
         Rock stomping
Rock 'em sock 'em

And so we lived with it
        the boiling spring run off
        which takes itself
        and many with
        the undertow
        "I figured I had bought the farm"
        the farm or the basilica dome

either or both
        receding
        leaving behind
        notes
        flayed of their moment

In the interview
        floodlight t.v. camera
           "we wish to be helped
              and left alone"
His face as he says this
        shocked frozen

                    the little carved head
                        of a Protestant martyr

"I'll bet you've seen him."
"Of course. I have eyes. It's sad"
"There's more. Want to see?"

A cough
            a thank you
                        a "fleshy patter" of applause.

We have built
        not to mention...
                a paralyzed cynicism...
                        or spectation...
a cabin in the woods
        your bio says you were reared here
                pictures formica counters
                        console color tv
                            fiberglass shower
                                shag carpet in "autumn leaf" pattern

Here is the birth place of "The New Man"
        or "a" new man
Repeat this segment
        until all acknowledge
                the image
an Express train
        hallucination

        "Really, just go with it.
                Stay calm. We'll have
                    in an hour
                            the results
                                            and

Watch this:
     honey sunlight,
         tidy streets,
             birds
                  unopposed happiness.

Individuals entering and leaving the population, some doing both, assume for a time the role of guest at the door of a host, unable to decide either way. There is music to be had, there is rest and tranquillity.

Too fine a blade to hold an edge,
     too many on the street.

Once a year, they parade
     past emergency rooms
         where the bullet
             and the blade
                 had their say.

"Can you squeeze water from this rock?"
"Do you want a slap?"
"Yes, right here."
"You disgust me."

Carp pond at twilight
ripple
     of risen mouth
embedded in cloud reflection

"She loves me, she loves me
I love her, love her
she I, she I,
agh!"

Had I known what I know now
     relapse, steep white chalk walls

       straight-jacketed, buckled
Not me, mind you, him
detention room door slamming midway on him
and her, catatonic
      the ward's living statue
ignoring all yet omniscient
of the unfoldment
What bribe enticed her from her pose?

As if hailing a cab
      steps off a ledge
          of a set back
             and plunges
                 hair upstreaming
                    crushing a cab's top.
Cabled to a crane
      and hoisted directly
          to its shoot on the flat black roof
             of its parent company.

The river has a say in its background
capacity, evoking consensus:
lavender and magenta cirrus
in a raspberry
      merging with blueberry
                    concoction.
He is loose in this vicinity
You can hear the hiss
      of his sleeve brushing against the hedge,
          his raincoat laden
             with his piece

Just the stumbling limping swagger
      says to me, great against
          the Hudson river sunset.

He travels by cadillac, "a boat"
      up the embankment highway
            makes his run across spans grandiose
                or utilitarian, and when he measures out
I get some
        the city
his people
        get some.
Some of him goes in the river,
      and the silt is stirred up
           so a cop in a copter spots him
                and dispatches a blue cop boat.
The divers in clumsy rubber
      wet suits feel for a man made object
           the size, shape and feel
                of a man, and in retrieving him
                  make him available for us
              speak for him as best they can,
          wet, panting, faces red-ovalled
      from the masks they have lifted
to face our gazes.

Only a momentary curiosity
shows, and then she boards. Bon voyage!

I am the star of the pigeons on this bench.
It is about to snow
      a jet scratches the atmosphere
      but that, too, leaves me cold.
A vine crosses along razor wire fencing
      blocks the view of the adjoining lot.
      Brown and green blades of ice-grass.

The urging of the street
says I'm hungry for you

I'm in a hurry, I'm pleased
I'm so angry could split your skull
        I'm looking forward to something.
The street is truly helpless
        and if one wanted it to, it
                would shut up. It could be persuaded
                        to "take out" a driver.

Begin with red.
        Linger in Amber

's arms
        which have tattoos
                like you wouldn't
that is
        dissimilar to any other
                in Venice Beach
She was a common biker "chick"
        The Phone:
"Yes?"
"Who is this?"
"You should know. You're calling me."
"Alessandro?"
"No."
"Oh. Sorry."
She was a common
        was a common
                a
friendship ensued, passing
green reflecting mile posts
until arriving
        tired them.
Investing in a motel's magic fingers
        they lapsed

quietly into
      chat about
           How many times?
She adjusted the color
      of the tv in the corner
           so the slopes
                of the Andes
                    glowed volcanically
              His cigarette died
          in the red blast of the screen
      they watched
in the room with red Andes.
****

2.

They were above reproach
      in their habits
           their apologies
                smeared the lipstick
around and around their oral cavities
unseemly
the quince tree in the gravel in the courtyard light
next to the broad, sleek buick
I swung open my drawing room window
      popped a brew
           held my tongue
      you could hear the crybabies
through plasterboard walls
      setting up gun deals

              Meanwhile, alone in her chariot
              pursues through clouds
              absolute stillness her temples
              her eyes straight

knowing the one she seeks
will fill the screen
the leading, though waning
wreck in the moon

A close knit fist
a clenched brow
perforations like mosquito bites
up her pale arm.

There is a degree of offense
in bucking, projecting
his jism
into the institution

Belatedly, reform
takes off,
the runway fair,
the windsocks slack
the single lights merge, veer
pull back from the design
Nothing from the air can compare
to the healing looks
expression
their quantity
at last
in kind
Demonstrations, manifestations
deliveries
my hand
my fingers between
your fingers
We're way too intelligent
to let

these floating sighs
be what they purport
        to be
green signs glowing at night

Wipe a tear, a dew gathereth
a crowd assembles, for most
of the period, they sit
on their hands, then as the tide turns
and approaches us on our blankets
with summer novels, we pick ourselves
up by the pink burned scruffs
and traipse around scrub pines
and bracken, apart from all
but the weather.

In the cubicles, clerks
"overcome their inhibitions"
as their eyes bulge:
quarters dropping into slots
and the individual cinemas
set the clerks in motion
in excess of company projections.
The will wilts in ten minutes
and $2.50.

You leave with the one who brought you,
then drop her home, and are back at the night spot
with the twin stuffed dobermans
adorning the floor, the ambiance
of the hall is of a bank vault.
Her tongue on the nape of your neck
stretches around to the jugular,
the roughness forcing a swallow.

But when B calls
to say her ex-boyfriend OD'd,
his nickname "The Walker" by fellow
mental warders because
he walked everywhere, "even through the ghetto"
your sister B worries that all her crazy best friends
are killing themselves. And she to her husband:
"Honey, you aren't going to kill yourself, are you?"
"No, dear."
And B worries about herself.
And about you, you wonder,
worried about yourself.

Over our heads
the nutcase in her tower
opens the day's news
and the newspaper ax
splits her
from crown to sex
and she slaps the paper shut
and calls a neighbor who answers with a look
to her husband that says
"cookoo."

"Aw, honey, I'm just a tongue-tied oaf, and, and what I mean to say, what
I mean is, I love you. There. I said it and I'm done. Except, will you marry
me? We can take my car, gas it up, and be man and wife by tonight, and
honey, you know that's what I wanted when I first set eyes on you. Will
you do it? Will you come with me?"

She repeated his words,
he memorized her expression.
And the TV went on.

CITY OF WATER

I wanted to go to the collapse site
catastrophe compressed into gray dust.
I wondered if I would see pieces
of someone.
I had an idea I could help put pieces back together.
Instead, I looked at photographs of the rubble,
but I saw nothing definitely human.
I thought I saw several vertebrae
spread out and squashed flat.
But I couldn't get close enough,
could not step through the window of the photo
to hold someone.
I was far enough away to miss the worst.
In bits and pieces, I heard and saw enough.
The plume of smoke showed me it was so.
A morgue-van dashing towards it did, too.
But now, I wish I could lie on that ground
and weep.

about the author

ROBERT THOMPSON is a Midwesterner who has lived in Brooklyn for the past twenty-five years. He studied poetry at Brooklyn College and wrote a Ph.D. dissertation on James Schuyler at The City University of New York Graduate Center. A chapbook entitled *The Pear Tree's Winter* was published by Intuflo/Groundwater Press (Hudson, New York). He works at Touro College, where he teaches English at the School of Career and Applied Studies.

OTHER TITLES FROM AHADADA

Ahadada Books publishes poetry. Preserving the best of the small press tradition, we produce finely designed and crafted books in limited editions.

Bela Fawr's Cabaret (David Annwn)   978-0-9808873-2-7

Writes Gavin Selerie: "David Annwn's work drills deep into strata of myth and history,. exposing devices which resonate in new contexts. Faithful to the living moment, his poems dip, hover and dart through soundscapes rich with suggestion, rhythmically charged and etymologically playful. Formally adventurous and inviting disjunction, these texts retain a lyric coherence that powerfully renders layers of experience. The mode veers from jazzy to mystical, evoking in the reader both disturbance and content. *Bela Fawr's Cabaret* has this recognisable stamp: music and legend 'Knocked Abaht a Bit', mischievous humour yielding subtle insight."

Age of the Demon Tools (Mark Spitzer)   978-0-9808873-1-0

Writes Ed Sanders: "You have to slow down, and absorb calmly, the procession of gritty, pointillist gnarls of poesy that Mark Spitzer wittily weaves into his book. Just the title, *Age of the Demon Tools*, is so appropriate in this horrid age of inappropriate technology—you know, corruptly programmed voting machines, drones with missiles hovering above huts, and mind reading machines looming just a few years into the demon-tool future. When you do slow down, and tarry within Spitzer's neologism-packed litanies, you will find the footprints of bards such as Allen Ginsberg, whose tradition of embedding current events into the flow of poesy is one of the great beacons of the new century. This book is worth reading if only for the poem 'Unholy Millenial Litany' and its blastsome truths."

Sweet Potatoes (Lou Rowan)   978-0-9781414-5-5

Lou Rowan . . . is retired, in love and charged. He was raised by horse breeders and went to Harvard and thus possesses an outward polish. But he talks like a radical, his speech incongruous with his buttoned-down appearance. *Golden Handcuffs Review*, the local literary magazine that Rowan founded and edits, is much like the man himself: appealing and presentable on the outside, a bit wild and experimental at the core.

Deciduous Poems (David B. Axelrod)   978-0-9808873-0-3

Dr. David B. Axelrod has published hundreds of articles and poems as well as sixteen books of poetry. Among his many grants and awards, he is recipient of three Fulbright Awards including his being the first official Fulbright Poet-in-Residence in the People's Republic of China. He was featured in Newsday as a "Star in his academic galaxy," and characterized by the New York Times as "a treat." He has shared the stage with such notables as Louis Simpson, X. J. Kennedy, William Stafford, Robert Bly, Allen Ginsburg, David Ignatow and Galway Kinnell, in performance for the U.N., the American Library Association, the Struga Festival, and hundreds more schools and public events. His poetry has been translated into fourteen languages and he is a frequent and celebrated master teacher.

Late Poems of Lu You (Burton Watson)   978-0-9781414-9-3

Lu You (1125–1210) whose pen name was 'The Old Man Who Does as He Pleases,' was among the most prolific of Chinese poets, having left behind a collection of close to ten thousand poems as well as miscellaneous prose writings. His poetry, often characterized by an intense patriotism, is also notable for its recurrent expression of a carefree enjoyment of life. This volume consists of twenty-five of Burton Watson's new translations, plus Lu You's poems as they appear in the original, making this a perfect collection for the lay reader as well as for those with a mastery of Song dynasty Chinese.

www.ahadadabooks.com

Oulipoems (Philip Terry)   978-0-978-1414-2-4

Philip Terry was born in Belfast in 1962 and has been working with Oulipian and related writing practices for over twenty years. His lipogrammatic novel *The Book of Bachelors* (1999), was highly praised by the Oulipo: "Enormous rigour, great virtuosity—but that's the least of it." Currently he is Director of Creative Writing at the University of Essex, where he teaches a graduate course on the poetics of constraint. His work has been published in *Panurge, PN Review, Oasis, North American Review* and *Onedit*, and his books include the celebrated anthology of short stories *Ovid Metamorphosed* (2000) and *Fables of Aesop* (2006). His translation of Raymond Queneau's last book of poems, *Elementary Morality*, is forthcoming from Carcanet. *Oulipoems* is his first book of poetry.

The Impossibility of Dreams (David Axelrod)   978-0-9781414-3-1

Writes Louis Simpson: "Whether Axelrod is reliving a moment of pleasure, or a time of bitterness and pain, the truth of his poetry is like life itself compelling." Dr. David B. Axelrod has published hundreds of articles and poems as well as sixteen books of poetry. Among his many grants and awards, he is recipient of three Fulbright Awards including his being the first official Fulbright Poet-in-Residence in the People's Republic of China . He was featured in *Newsday* as a "Star in his academic galaxy," and characterized by the *New York Times* as "A Treat." His poetry has been translated into fourteen languages and he is a frequent and celebrated master teacher.

Now Showing (Jim Daniels)   0-9781414-1-5

Of Jim Daniels, the *Harvard Review* writes, "Although Daniels' verse is thematically dark, the energy and beauty of his language and his often brilliant use of irony affirm that a lighter side exists. This poet has already found his voice. And he speaks with that rare urgency that demands we listen." This is affirmed by Carol Muske, who identifies the "melancholy sweetness" running through these poems that identifies him as "a poet born to praise".

China Notes & The Treasures of Dunhuang (Jerome Rothenberg)   0-9732233-9-1

"*The China Notes* come from a trip in 2002 that brought us out as far as the Gobi Desert & allowed me to see some of the changes & continuities throughout the country. I was traveling with poet & scholar Wai-lim Yip & had a chance to read poetry in five or six cities & to observe things as part of an ongoing discourse with Wai-lim & others. The ancient beauty of some of what we saw played out against the theme park quality of other simulacra of the past....A sense of beckoning wilderness/wildness in a landscape already cut into to serve the human need for power & control." So Jerome Rothenberg describes the events behind the poems in this small volume—a continuation of his lifelong exploration of poetry and the search for a language to invoke the newness and strangeness both of what we observe and what we can imagine.

The Passion of Phineas Gage & Selected Poems (Jesse Glass)   0-9732233-8-3

The Passion of Phineas Gage & Selected Poems presents the best of Glass' experimental writing in a single volume. Glass' ground-breaking work has been hailed by poets as diverse as Jerome Rothenberg, William Bronk and Jim Daniels for its insight into human nature and its exploration of forms. Glass uses the tools of postmodernism: collaging, fragmentation, and Oulipo-like processes along with a keen understanding of poetic forms and traditions that stretches back to Beowulf and beyond. Moreover, Glass finds his subject matter in larger-than-life figures like Phineas Gage—the man whose life was changed in an instant when an iron bar was sent rocketing through his brain in a freak accident—as well as in ants processing up a wall in time to harpsichord music in order to steal salt crystals from the inner lip of a cowrie shell. The range and ambition of his work sets it apart. The product of over 30 years of engagement with the avant-garde, *The Passion of Phineas Gage & Selected Poems* is the work of a mature poet who continues to reinvent himself with every text he produces.

www.ahadadabooks.com